FLU *in the* TIME *of* ALLERGIES

FLU *in the* TIME *of* ALLERGIES

Juan Parra

RESOURCE *Publications* · Eugene, Oregon

FLU IN THE TIME OF ALLERGIES

Resource Publications
An Imprint of Wipf and Stock Publishers
199 W. 8th Ave., Suite 3
Eugene, OR 97401

www.wipfandstock.com

PAPERBACK ISBN: 978-1-6667-3689-2
HARDCOVER ISBN: 978-1-6667-9574-5
EBOOK ISBN: 978-1-6667-9575-2

MARCH 16, 2022 11:37 AM

Contents

Power Outages

My Dad played the guitar.
My mother lighted candles and tiptoed with her eyes closed.
These sequences of power outages and music went on for a long time.
One minute I was naming the dogs that licked Saint Lazarus' knees,
The next I was screaming for my life, submerged in darkness.

It was the twentieth power outage that month.
My mother no longer tiptoed but glided gracefully across the living room
Candle in one hand, eyes tightly shut. My father strummed the guitar and sang
Of angels crucifying communists, or oranges falling in love with naughty lemons,
Or the satire of Stalin's portrait in our empty refrigerator. But on some nights,
He sang feebly like a child turning old as parasites conjured dark magic
From the carcass of the homeless dog who always sought to look you in the eyes.

I sat in front of them
In a world that now seemed too normal for the abnormality of light
In the tear, that night shed.
Father strummed the guitar.
Mother perfected her glide.
I sat in front of them, each night, more and more in love.
This went on for a long time.

TV Show

I was lucky to have a picture of General Franco
When Nixon abducted me.
America, I whispered at the TV, even in this modern age you're so wild.

No, I take it back.

You are a beauty queen at the doors of a cemetery
Sniffing cocaine from the chin of an ape.
You stand by me in my darkest hour with your artificial light,
You shake your ass to destress me and show me a good time.

No More I love You's

I was wearing my blonde wig
When Trump pulled me over.

America my love, I thought I knew you.
But you're living so wild now:
Bowing like Franco. Dancing like Mussolini.
Smiling like Pinochet. Clapping like Stalin.
I thought you loved me.
Once upon a time you would wink at me
And would whisper: "Becquer and Lorca," in my ear.

"I'm gonna need you to step out of the car," Trump said while his upper lip
twitched.
"No more I love you's is right," he said, as he aggressively turned off the
stereo.
"I'm gonna need you to balance yourself on your thumbs for the next ten
minutes.
That better not be a wig your wearing, your tongue better not be having
love affairs with
Other dialects."

Thirty seconds later

My thumbs cracked under the pressure of my fat limbs,
Forcing me to give up Moliere, hiding under my tongue. To point towards
Tchaikovsky crying of terror in my ear. Conned into admitting my love for
Bashevis and everything Yiddish.
My poor wig prayed and endured under the stomps of an enraged Tyrant.

"You're not real. From the vomit your tongue stinks of, you probably don't
love my People," Trump Raged, while he hauled me from my ears and
crammed me in his policeman's hat.

Now, straightforwardly, no more swans. Or dances on rose petals. Or
sentimental education. No more Poets and love affairs. No more Romance
before sunrise; let's talk of ethnicity Diplomas, of bans and Tariffs, of
odious men in white robes talking Nazism and looking
Ominous on centric Boulevards. America my love you are so wild: There
are no more I love you's for me,
In your heart."

ONCE UPON A TIME

"Everybody knows what happened between Fidel Castro and me."
Said my grandfather. We were playing a game of chess
And the winner would get to eat the last can of pork and beans.
The match unfortunately would always end in a deadlock.
I remember Raul was our only spectator, and he
Would always wear a t-shirt that said, 'Moscow boys drive me wild.'
Finally, after five days, I let Fidel win when he begged in private
That he was so hungry, he had started to eat the lice
That were having orgies in his beard.

IX Cuban Recollections

I

I played with scissors before bedtime
Pretending they were action heroes.

II

Father was busy negotiating with the colony of ants
To return the crumbs of bread they stole.

III

The blonde saint in his bathrobe was always smiling
Except when the dog ran into the room
Wearing a black beret.

IV

Castro wore gold dentures and so did Reagan.

V

We bit hard on desiccated fish.

VI

"The pope stole the happiness from my dreams,"
Confided my uncle.

VII

"The world's tallest giraffe was going to catapult me towards
God," said my aunt.

VIII

At the end of the hall the old widow transformed children
Into pigs.

IX

Mother sprinkled the morning tears on the porcelain Buddha.

MARTYR

I'm the last communist faithful.
It's been Forty-Four years since Mao's
Death, and I still cry in front of his
Portrait. The parks are
Full of Tai Chi practitioners.
Havana's decomposed dreams make
My nostrils itch. A woman missing an arm
Offers to sell me a portion of her nipple,
And I don't even know her. One day, America
Will swim towards Havana and I will swim
In the opposite direction.
I have a plastic knife.
I'll use it to shave my beard, which is seven feet long.

Unforgiven

Grandma Fefi was so old she didn't wear her dentures anymore.
I stopped visiting when I turned eighteen. The corridor that led to
Her house remained in the same disrepair as I remember it, and
As I traversed it, conjured the memory of my cat's tragic
Face that at that moment was as handsome as ever with long
Dashing whiskers, as it looked up from a pool of blood that stained
His soft black fur, his gut unfastened and intestines hanging, "They
Butchered my poor cat granny," I screamed and agonized. But she was
Busy painting blonde the bold head of her porcelain Buddha.
The cat remained lucid for a few minutes in which he even tried to whisk
Away with his tongue the flies that started to settle on his intestines.

The house was old and screaming for repairs. I knocked on the door and
it dented in. The tiles were cracked all over, and there was a stench of sour
armpits and dust that jabbed my nostrils. Grandma Fefi was also a mess: She
kissed me and left a line of saliva on my cheeks; her arms were emaciated,
and wore a long robe that had dirty, gold stars drawn on it. "There's a strong
smell in here Grandma," I said. "It's the fucking cats peeing everywhere,"
She answered. "They're still upset I left the door opened the day Jecki was
massacred. They've disrespected this house one piss at a time along with
fights and orgies." "But I don't think these cats know about Jecki; it's been
more than ten years," I said. "I'm telling you these bitches are dragging that
shit from past generations. I've tried to apologize in every way possible."

The smell didn't let me sleep that night. I walked back and forth only stopping
to gaze out the window. Then out of nowhere, I heard a loud sound. I saw
grandma holding an old kerosene lantern barely lit, a small pigeon tangled
in her long greasy hair, and the porcelain Buddha crushed in front of a
clowder of cats. They looked like they wanted to rip her to shreds. It was so
much hate that even facing one of them, would have drowned me in fear.

BACALAO

They hung for days.
Altering from brawn to carcass,
And scant for the warring flies
Slaughtering each other to feast on its
Salty rinds. They were stinky, ugly,
Like a pair of aliens that died of love for a rat,
Or something Caliban would trim Prospero's toenail for.

My father pulled out their guts
And drowned them in salt and vinegar.
His hands stung from the acidity of the vinegar, and the roughness of the
salt.
I stared at his old hands that with age looked like a set of skinny and
Sour pieces of rind.

A week before my mother decided to leave.
"I'm way too young;" she would tell him after months of plastic surgery
and
Late outings. That week my father resumed alcoholism for the first time in
thirty years.
I wanted to tell him that there were a bunch of people in this world that
thought too
Much of themselves and too little of mortality and that they sucked. That
most of the time
We are not as amazing as we think but rather live in the constant cradle of
the highlight reel. But he was so old, so wrinkled that I could not bring my
self
To say these things to someone so mature, experienced, desiccated in
time.

He hung the carcasses once again.
Vinegar dripped down from the dead.
Their heads were disfigured, eyeless.
I sat alone in the backyard.

I wished my dad knew that I loved him.
I sat staring at them.
And the Bacalao stared back

BACALAO TWIST

They hung for days
Altering from brawn to carcass.
The warring flies slaughtered each other
To feast on its salty cadaver.
They looked like a pair of aliens that died of love for a rat
Or something for which Caliban would trim Prospero's toenail.
My father pulled on their guts and drowned them in salt and vinegar.
His hands stung from the acidity of the vinegar, and the roughness of the
salt.
I stared at his old hands that with age looked like thin and sour pieces of
peel.

A week before my mother decided to leave.
"I'm still young;" she told him after months of plastic surgery and late
outings.

That week my father resumed alcoholism after a long pause.
I felt sorry for him.
I felt like telling him that there were a bunch of people in this world that
thought too much of Themselves and too little of mortality and that they
sucked. That most of the time we are not as Awe-Inspiring as we believe
but instead live in the constant cradle of the highlight reel. But he Was
Old, so Wrinkled that I could not bring myself to say these things to
someone so mature And Desiccated in time.

And yet, I pitied a bunny when I remembered a fox's past:

There were times when mom's legs were a mass of punctured woes, and
dad would turn away, And with eyes closed, draw a cross of vinegar on her
forehead as if he could magically cure Diabetes; or the times that dad and
I played Spaniards and Indians, and he would never run out Of bullets;
or When dad danced rough with mom out of jealousy; or when witches
would make Him disappear only to return him, out of love, smelling of
rum, and with loose fists.

11

That was all, too, fucked up dad.

He hung the carcasses once again.
Vinegar dripped down from the dead.
I sat alone in the backyard.
I stared at them,
And the Bacalao stared back.

Animal

I was so poor I had to walk the street hunting for cats to eat.
I would spend my time with the neighborhood dogs.
I could hear their growling bellies.
"I've been fucking starving since Gorbachev sucked Reagan's cock."
An old dog barked at me.
Months passed. My mother was wearing a shirt that said,
"Cat lover." I stumbled upon her while I was hunting,
And she pretended not to know me.

At the Center of The Universe

They are done drying the morning tears on the Pope's navel.
The false Christ enjoyed drowning the newborn kitties,
Except the ones that sucked on his toes mistaking it for a nipple.
The commandant was busy murdering the lice in his beard.
Raul jiggled his ass to Pitbull and so did Bush.
"They stole the secrets that thrived in the cornucopia of my ears,"
Cried my father.
"I'll teach rats the art of dancing on one leg,"
Said the stripper who swore loved me.
In the square the men threw roses at the white doves.
O to cry naked on the sofa before the comedy act
Or to make love while reading a porn magazine.
I crowned my black cat with the thorns of roses you left me,
Dark meadow.

War Under Your Eyelids

You plot war under your eyelids.
You punish me with cantos of dark magic
And images of doves stained with wine.
All Day long you paint the clouds grey in the nucleus of Spring.

You waterboard the homeless cat that roams tormented and fatigued
Feebly raking the floor like a farmer looking for heaven under dry and
withered crops.
You lock the poor animal in a cage with a sparrow and pretend
indifference at massacres
And genocides. The flies that settle on the shredded carcass, you scurry
away, almost as if
Remorse is mesmerizing your heart. But you plot more war under your
eyelids.

An army trudges over your face and carve emotions based on
Fictions you created. And suddenly, after the third day,
The sparrow springs up with a beard on its beak and long elegant feathers,
And you rest stunned at the miracle that is love.
You admit; how foolish to suffer grey skies in the nucleus of Spring.

Babalawo Ceremony in The Central Dome

They are plucking the sins from the caged dove,
And grinding the rooster's dead body
To accelerate the trickle of blood
That crashes on the methodically polished linoleum
Whose soul's whispers echoes against the vaulted
Ceiling, and dampers before the horror of rotten pig's
Ears, and Jesus floating in a cup of spiced rum.

The black Madonna shakes her ass.
The white dresses are stained rough in gashes of blood.
The figures move back and forth
In a trance like formation, releasing the ashes of cigars
That had orgies in their mouths, out to the world
Rushing every corner and rubbing against every
Mortar saint, leaving no witness, untouched.

Against the Red Light

I liked Soviet cartoons.
Every time my father turned the T.V off
I would turn the T.V back on.
This struggle went on for some time.
One minute I was laughing at the bunny ears protruding from Stalin's hat
The next I was kneeling in front of a wooden, gleeful Christ
Reading a bible infested with book lice.

It was my father's birthday.
My mother boiled a pig's heart
And hoarded the fat she trimmed for future celebrations.
My father spoke to his friends about the absurd
Stare of Marxism and gave Lenin credit for inventing hunger.

I sat by the window, defeated
Reconciled with the darkness streaming from the T.V
Replacing it with the row of feeble streetlamps,
That carried my eyes into a pitch darkness of a future
I was lucky never to be lost in.

August

They are sewing arms on dead doves
And hearts rot on meat hooks,
While tears sprout withered flowers
At the gates of Babylon.

The pungent, windless August piles
Naked cadavers with a deviant
Smile, released to the world
Spoiling the ceremonial food,
Owed to the dead.

LIKE THIS I REMAIN

I am still an immigrant.
It's been thirty years since,
And I'm still the tear that drowned the Havana coastline.
The rough waters, and the stench of vomit still blemish my fingers.
There's a blind man that offers me a Superman doll, but I'm too wrinkled
To play with toys.

Castro and Pinochet hammer down my big toe dressed as Jesuits
In the nightmare they conjured.
I have a rusty machete; I'll use it to cut the fields of grass,
Which are miles and miles long.

STAGES

You were terrifying to be around
From time to time:
When you spoke in tongues
With a bible open on your legs
And a lunatic grin
Whenever you swayed back and forth
Wearing a black beret so large it would smother your forehead.

You were tender to be around
From time to time:
When you offered shredded coco and chocolate
To our afternoon readings of Nicolas Guillen.

And once again

You were terrifying to be around
From time to time:
When you covered your face with your hands
While drowning in a sob and cursing Reagan for spitting
In your eyeballs.

You were so tender to be around
From time to time:
When Mon wore your pants and you
Her dress,
While floating on a moon lit dance floor.

And

You were tender to be around
From time to time:
When you consoled the sobbing kitties
Whose mother melted in the orange canvas
Of a bloodshot sunset.

But

You were horrifying:

That time;
When you became enraged
At the hungry kitties whose screams
You drowned
One by one,
In a bathtub of scalding water.

I'm staring at you daddy, dancing in a void
Wearing patterns of smiles and tears.
Your smile, like a flower that covers the mud
As your tears soften the earth: a world
You can't control;
That realm where you give so much and
Seize a lot, impulsively.

The fragile stages of my growth
Slowly metabolizing in my heart
As you sink
In the movable clay that is age.
Once you cease to exist, I will feel nothing
And yet so much,
Like an angel born a pauper.

Flu in the Time of Allergies

Pluck our eyebrows in the dark
Stare at the horizon, that place where
Another place is born away from our dark corner

Yield.
Digg furrows and
Lick each other's knees and elbows in our dark corner

Dance.
Cast voodoo spells on the rotten berries,
Love me in our dark corner

Grind the dead skin from the souls of my feet on my shadow.
Incite nightmares to suicide using our umbilical cords
In our dark corner

Sneeze prudently so as not to wake the doves
Sleeping on the homeless dog,
And kill the fever with a cold shower in our dark corner

Hold your breath.
Transform from flesh to ashes, from ashes to specter.
Play like old people disguised as happy in our dark corner.

The morning that is born
Lame, heels broken, bruised limps
Hush its tears and lure it
To our dark corner.

GAME OF CHESS

The king moves frighten,

In my father's wrinkled grip.

Mao Superstar

I rubbed Mao's fat cheeks
Praying for a cow to fall from the sky.

The witch down the hall caressed my father's swollen feet
Without my mother knowing.

I rubbed Mao's cheeks
Praying for daddy's feet to never swell again.

Mother added a kiss on my forehead to my mornings,
And pulled on my cheeks until she molded a fatigued smile on my face.
Mother gave so much love.

I kept rubbing Mao's cheeks
Asking that they never leave me.

On the happy days,
daddy joked and showed mercy to the colony of ants that invaded the
kitchen,
And exiled the roaches that had orgies on my bed.
Mom would put on The Beatles and made daddy stay home.
He was happy to stay, too.

I rubbed Mao's cheeks praying the day would never end.

And then one day Mao was shattered in pieces in the living room,
And Mom told me his name was Buddha. Mao was the name
Of the communist that dad made fun of.

I sat in front of crows wearing long robes,
Who mediated the shouting bouts between mom and dad,
And ordered me to pick who I loved most.

I waved goodbye at a man with swollen feet.

I called for him as he pretended not to hear, and became part of the masses.
I took hard breaths and for a long time never prayed again.

Johnny On the Rocks

On that night
I urinated so much the toilet overflowed,
Drafted peace treaties for my warring cats,
Shaped my mustache like Tsar Nicky,
Iced the ear I bit off from the memory
That jabbed my gut.

I Fished Christ out of my facet
Bating him with my son's umbilical cord,
Read self-help books high on Coffee and guava pastries,
Listened to songs, fell in a trumpet's bell,
Traded sucking on Eden's tits for a woman's nipple.

And then I was distracted by Buddha disguised as Mao Zedong
Waving a mini iPod in one hand, and gold dentures in the other,
Donning a toothless mouth where Rasputin shampooed
Marx's thick, lice infected beard.

But then I really lost it when I heard the drumming of stilettos
Seducing the linoleum. A woman's busty body,
Like one crafted in a teenager's horny dream
Her perfect accent- one that's never been uprooted
Drowning any hope of salvation in the pupil of her eyes:
So sinful even trees moved to night orgies and broken hearts
Until I tired and started to worry about life, and my thinning hair.

Waiting for Superman

1

The raft was jammed.
My sister hugged her bible.
I begged my mother for a Superman Action figure
As soon as we get to America.
"Make sure to vomit outside," she would whisper to me.
That summer tasted of salt water and vomit.
The heat made our pores throb.
My father worried for our tired, sad limbs.

2

A tempest formed in the distance.
The wind rapped hard on our faces.
Our hopes were smashed to crumbs.

3

"Pray to whoever will save us and repent later," cried my sister.
We were nothing but human crumbs on a colossus dappled with spew.
Jabbing breaths raked my lungs; saliva crawled up from my exhausted
glands
Flooding my mouth with puke, forcing my cheeks to bloat before release
Leading to another cycle of hard breaths like a Christ on the cross,
Nails crushing his hands, his feet, his blessed emaciated feet.

4

My mother held on to me as if I was going to turn into a memory,
A tear claiming a heaven won by default of age,

A past, a future not realized, a child stripped from her arms by malicious waves,
A pile of clothes drenched in urine and puke,
A collection of shredded limbs, a wrinkled face with thinning hair
No longer asking for Superman, but for an assurance of life, she could not grant.

Soot

Death crushed pillows
On the faces
Of sleeping babies.
The world was a vast graveyard
For vultures to play.
We were smothered like sardines
Against others
Just like us.
The children cried for the macarons
They ate in their dreams.
We traded tears as we
Turned into soot.
The sky was soiled
With the cadavers
Of angels.

Swayed to A Bow

On the hunchbacked ocean
The stench of feces baptizes itself in my nostrils.
I wrap my arms around my skinny ribs.
My mother massages my face with her wrinkled hands
As the distance grows
From that shattered canvas that is Cuba,
Host to inverse pyramids and poverty.

You're near.
I untangle your limps from my body.
I remember the threads of hair I lost
To your rage against gravity.
I try to exorcise our goodbye from my memory,
The kisses and screams, that fester in that recent history
You, praying to saints
Tring to make them
Stir and bend their clay torsos
To the night's howl and the shattered neck of doves.

What are you doing?
When will I seen you again?
You, whose beauty is a neon light
In a power outage
So intense
Even in blindness
I would see you.

You hide in my gut and
Stir my fancy.
You dance on my palms in a second of lust.
You are not left behind.
You are real.

I imagine you
Far away
M'I still embroidered in your future?
Do you still see us tenderizing our wrinkles
With hickory and Palo Santo?

The city lights are drowned under
The oppressive weight of darkness.

Nostalgia.
God.
Devil.
Perdition and light are what you are
On this disheveled vessel that begrudgingly
Carries our human crumbs of bodies.
The birth of Venus
Destined to drown in a gray, zealous tempest,
A pressure that sways me, to a bow.

ROBERTO GIVING BIRTH

Roberto slipped on the pool deck and landed on the back of his head, cracked it wide open. Pedro drilled his arm in Roberto's head and slammed it in and out like if he was arm fucking the back of Roberto's head until he pulled out a hare. "People like to fuck the thought that the world is ending," Pedro said. "Don't worry, the world is not going to end so soon," Roberto replied. When the paramedics arrived, they said that the wound was not as bad. "What about the rabbit, Pedro, pulled out of my head?" Roberto asked. Everybody looked shocked because Roberto is, for the most part, a sane man. "Roberto," I said, "The fall is making you a little feverish." "When I was sitting on the ground, I felt Pedro's arm inside my head, and he pulled out a rabbit. He showed it to me while he held it from its ears," he said. "Is this normal?" I asked the paramedics. "Not really, but it's not rare for people to act a little wacky after falling on the head," one of the paramedics answered. I concluded that Roberto was just confused. But Roberto, when he returned to work, began asking me to suggest names for a rabbit. He spoke with such certainty that I didn't dare contradict him. He would always say to me how smart his rabbit was and how proud he felt. Eventually, Roberto started wearing a headband that read, "proud parent of a cute bunny rabbit". His joy was so expansive, that I started to feel hatred at how happy he was, every time he walked by me.

At Home

One night while curling my whiskers and licking myself,
Only pausing these pleasures to sharpen my nails
Against the tattered sofa in the darkest corner of the house,
Maggie rushed past me with her parrot
That popped the pimples behind her ears,
Both rushing and hollering to be on time for something,
Except the old dog who stared at the ceiling.

"What a fucking spectacle of a ceiling," I said mockingly.
"The stars are hiding," said the old dog, and cried corny notes such as:
"O my honey love, my lips are dry, cracked, and withered
By your betrayal."
And read my paws without permission:
"You're stuck in a horny spell," he said

I was relieved.
I thought he would tell me
I'll go nuts and slash Maggie's parrot to shreds
While dragging his bloody carcass all over the house.
Or end up strapped to a bed crazy as a cuckoo bird,
Unable to say or do anything to the priest holding a cross
On my forehead while speaking in tongues.

Instead, there I was, horny and soaked in tears
Staring at this old being as he observed the ceiling
And sobbed uncontrollably. I could no longer support his grief
And summed up the strength to shout, "Man, don't fucking cry
For a slutty ass, trash loving, poor excuse of a bitch."
But he was heartbroken. It was late and pitch dark.
Since there was nothing else, I could have said, I walked to my ragged sofa,
Unable to hold my tears, before falling asleep.

WAR

When we floated across
No fish was without sword or shield.
The gentle blue of the Caribbean
Was drowning in blood and floating heads
That spooked the crumbs of peace left in
Our hearts.
The elegant and flashy fish scales bowed to a savagery
Sewn in our hearts before creation's first words.

Mackerels and Barracudas floated with big holes on their stomachs
And the lucky few to just lose an eye or a fin, suffered from blood clots in
their brains.
Our pores were on fire, but we still prayed for our bony torsos.
Our lips were purple, and our skins faded into a yellow shade of rotting.
We were nothing but the creation of humanity's ingenious past time.

TSELA

Your eyes are the flogging to my gut.
Your smile the thief of my stare,
Callous yet thrilling.
The way we function
Is by resistance lessened
Increased and played with,
Twisting when you
Twist in me
Your teeth butchering
My entrails
My gut flaked
Into convoluted lumps of flesh,
Vicious and vivid.
The way we function
Is primitive,
Flirting on
Our private crust of universe,
Wanting and letting,
Drowning and gasping
For the hour, winks, lip movements
Codes.

I enjoy the fancy of your naked
Brown nipples, soft, full, well-formed
Distant borders of exile.
I believe me astray;
weight down in
The caramel of your sweet pupils.
I believe you.
I believe in your steps
Past me, the back of your head
Jabs of regret.

In a ritual of pain
I'm prying you from my gut
While rubbing lard on my bony rib cage,
Lubricating the dryness,
The miscarriage of another Eve
Suffocated under sternum and cartilage.
My barren, coward ribs unworthy of
Labor, and carnations.

CORPSE

For Modesto Perez

Stitch my kisses on your cheeks.
Blame the wind's playfulness
On ghosts and saints.
Walk without permission from life.

We have mutated into goodbyes.
You a skeletal muteness,
Me, orphaned, plucking my thinning hair
In Humanity's gut.

You spit steps at the floor.
You drag your carcass
Soiling with your rotten stock
The whimpering linoleum.

Your ribcage forms echoing caves
Of bones and raped flesh by time's
Fury and your lack of self-preservation.
Your yellow, rotting skin proves to you,
You are dying.

Or already dead?
Today is a dark canvas:
Swans eating each other's intestines.
Vultures nibbling on nipples,
Rotting in piles and piles of cadavers.
Your lungs skinny and shrunken, hauling
Its nicotine passions.

We are drowning in the hour life inundated for us.
Even in love there is pain.
Hiding in a future far from your death
I feel pain when mom scrubs your feeble carcass,
And reminds you, of how much,
We love you.

RED STAR

I find my mother hugging a photograph of me.
In the photograph, I'm wearing a black beret and carrying a rifle.
I tell her I've never worn a beret or even held a rifle.
I'm smoking a cigar and sporting thick facial hair.
My mother insists that that's me in the photograph. I have never smoked
A cigar and I shave every day. The red star pinned on the beret I'm
wearing
Makes me look like a Marxist revolutionary. I steal the photograph and
hide it in
My safe to examine it whenever I want. I must admit that if I take away
the beret and facial
Hair, he looks just like me. The resemblance troubles me. Maybe that's
who I used to be.
Now I'm not sure who I am.

DAY AND NIGHT

O lingering memories that stalk me,
I won't deny me the pleasure, the succulence,
From time to time, without the slightest warning
To feel overjoyed and easy.

The days spent
Dancing a ceremonial dance for sunshine
Under the almond trees,
With my dear Katie dancing by my side.

Until the night summons us
To turn on the kerosene lamp,
And shepherd a clowder of cats through the darkness.
I hypnotize them with flute and Katie with song,
As we are careful not to drown in the flooded hollows,
Of yesterday's rain.

A Day in 1993

1

The morning was swaddled in vomitus and urine,
And tears that sprouted dead flowers in my mother's heart.
A child, absolved of innocence,
Submissively, urinating on himself,
Nomadically, floating on a ragged raft,
Too old and too tired,
Red and raw on the sun's grill.

2

Mother
I'm fearful of the lullaby you hum to me.
I'm troubled by the fragile surface that gleams
Dark blue and ill-omened,
The wind that jabs my eyes,
The salt that clogs my pores,
Your song numbing my ear
With a sedative quality,
A rehearsal to stillness
And muteness.

BROKEN SPHERE

My cat kills in my honor every morning.
A belligerent stench crawls from the refrigerator
And plays on my nostrils with malicious glee.
A stew cooks slowly on top of a greasy, dirty grill,
And Sunlight filters through the cracked window blinds
Slowly suffocating in the heavy cloud of smoke that grips the kitchen.

I throw a grenade in the lake and collect bits and pieces of fish for paella.
I sit in front of the mirror worrying about the thinness of my hair.
I argue about nihilism like a true Karamazov with the termites on my
book cabinet
And help ants pilfer grains of rice. My dog sits on top of her newborn cubs
Until they're crushed, every time she gives birth.
I dig the graves; they see me sob once a year.

I bear a black feather, two broken families,
A friend's bible, the memory of a lover who jabbed herself
Underneath the nails with a sewing needle, hours of heartache.
Light pollution has denied me, the pleasure of stars.

My Apartment on 65th and Collins

I suffered in my little studio.
Once a month an old compartment maid stuffed my pillow
With lethargies of grey hair;
But most of the time, it was solitude.
Each corner with its own set of mice
Reading detective novels in complete taciturnity,
Biting themselves whenever their lips tried to shudder
From the oppressive rhythm, silence so egotistical
I would hear ants drowning in my leftover spirit.

Except when the flamenco dancers next door made love.
They would scream "I love you" but in reality
It was more like deviant, pornographic sex.
Their dance studio was on the corner of 60th and Collins
Where I sometimes strolled away from the sounds of loving,
Except that time, when I decided to stay but ended up crying
Like a starving child. So bitterly I wept,
I thought, for a moment, that they were weeping with me.

PARAISO TROPICAL

Saint Lazarus is drinking a Wernesgruner and sporting speedos,
While his dogs perform improvised poetry with the words baby and
milkshake
To the lovers who paint whiskers on each other's torsos.
It's freezing.
On the grey horizon, I see Mary no longer tear-drenched, but red fedora
on head,
Making "cool dude" gestures and back flipping on a surfboard.
The beach is grey.
Even Castro would be cold and quiet.
Even Lamartine would have accepted the red flag.
"You see we also have beaches in Germany," says the swan that whispers
fantasies in my ear.
I walk on the sand to what looks like mangroves and find an orgy of
raccoons:
"Oh, yeh baby," screams a raccoon to the one licking his toenail and
"I'm going to fall for you Maggie" to the other that scratches his belly.

I point my cross at them and ask Christ to keep me now more than ever,
As the waves threatened to crash violently before finding their composure
On the soft sand, that keeps the secret history of the dead,
Buried, and my toes ignorant of their suffering.

Empires

Buddha.
Forgive the intrusion of my little finger
On your porcelain forehead,
My mother's wrath and the anger
I conjured, in our living room.

I was born in an iron pot
Where empires mixed my race.
Where Batistas and Machados, Castros and Guevaras,
Nikitas and Nixons, Francos and Mussolinis share each other's
Dentures in front of a starving children that plucked the worms that
Fester in their bellies as bait for fish.
I'm an uncoordinated patterns of colors,
Uprooted from the sanity of individuality,
A red iron curtain that rips the eyes off the blue whisper overwhelming
The light pastel now screaming at its weeping wrists,
The identity inside my body withered in brown marrying gray.

Buddha.
Just cut me down in pieces and feed me to pigs
For the intrusion of my childish finger,
That time when I wrecked your porcelain forehead.
Bring forth the wrath of empires, that baton
Made for the undesired, awkward people of this world,
Destined to hushed and lamed limbs.

HEAT WAVE TRAGEDY

The days
That jabbed their tongue in my ears:
My father's
Mood swings
Sewn on my mother's forehead.
My mother's
Lover
Wailing in the pantry.
The dog's
Decaying organs
Wishing they could still make love.
Heat waves and power outages.

Roaches
Moon walking
Pranking the blind cat.
Ants
Diving into
The lit kerosene lamps.
Sour armpits
Festering in sweat.
I raked the barren ground
With the heels of my tiny feet.

Rats
Moon bathing
Poking each other's souls.
The crucified mannequin
Donning a red beret
Singing
Of poets and muses
Of pearls and thieves.

The night's omnipotent jaw
Crushing the exhausted
Flame
We worshipped for light
Swallowing us whole.
I raked the barren ground
With the heels of my tiny feet.

My Twenty-Seventh Birthday

I spent the morning searching for meaning under my grandfather's wig,
And licked the wisdom from his brazen scalp. I brainstormed for solutions
to the disloyalty towards my lover, and my wife. Offered Roses, and feathers
from the Chickens I drowned in my bathtub, and even the toe Videla nailed
to my nipple in a dream, to the porcelain Buddha whose forehead I cracked
with a kiss.

In the afternoon I poured bourbon in my café au lait
And tried voodoo chants on the almond tree that died of love.
I argued with my grandmother that angels also get their palms read.
I wore white, and whistled to the parrots that were busy planning
The revolution against the white doves that monopolized
All the rum.

In the evening my mother interpreted my dreams before dinner
And my father taught me how to dance expressionless.
Later that night, I ate the crumbs my lover left on the table.
And much later in the night,
I woke up and spied my wife while she prayed for fire and floods,
For love and miracles: for the almond tree to resurrect, and never die
again.

DOUCHKO

My dear cat is watching me so serious. "Is that Cabernet or Merlot?" He
asks me.
His whiskers disheveled as he continues to jab me with his gaze. "No
Douchko, it's just cranberry juice." I say. "Christ is drowning in your
bathtub, sobbing for Romeo and Juliet.
Is he not as tasty as the wine you're drinking?" Once again, I reassure
him that it's just cranberry juice. "And love? Talk to me about love. Did
he not get his ass whoop for love?" "I guess, Douchko. I guess I'm spoiled
and worthless," I say. "You can still pull him out. You can still save him."
He rushes me. I get up from the chair my father carved in the image
of Mayakovsky and open my drawer of miscellaneous items. From the
bottom of a crowded bunch, I pull out my son's umbilical cord to use like
rope. Douchko smirks. His whiskers looking longer and more elegant
than ever. I hysterically run to the bathroom and reach the bathtub. Then:
"Douchko, where the fuck did he go" I screamed. "I got you!" He says
mockingly and does Vallejo: "'Love is a sinful Christ,' Juancito. He died
days ago. He died of love. He just sunk quietly and died."

The Things

She carried
Her son's ashes in a black beret
The rose she rescued from suffocating in the mud
The halo she stole from the tired priest
A canvas of shadows
The path carved by her lover's hands
The seconds lost to yawning
The angel wings she sewed on the ragged doll
The cats that keep her company in her dreams
The ceremonial dagger she uses to trim
The laments, of her past

You and I
Once
Lost in Each Other

I drowned canaries
In the sink.
You always won
Our staring duels.

We raked our skins with a metal sponge
Until skinny,
Baited the hungry possum with desiccated sardines,
Made vinegar crosses on our foreheads
Before nightfall.

We crucified the moon
On the back of our dawns,
Wrapped the crying knees
Of the porcelain Christ
In banana leaves.

We took turns wearing the crown of barbwire,
Stolen,
From the Babalawo priest,
Blew cigar rings at our faces
With the lights out.

We were lost
In each other's paper maze,
You with a hammer
And me with nails,
Squirmed
At the tip of the nail
That stretched and crushed our limbs.

We unlit candles
With our tongues,
Tamed our rabid, adrenaline
Infested breathing
In each other's arms,
As we begged each other for rest.

MATI

For: Matei Juanov Parra

I'm saving for you
The peace of prayers.
Sparks of flames.
The yawns before dreams.
The goodbye I fret over.
My fatigued neurons.
My desire for life.
The happy mornings
The tired evenings.
The caramel in my eyes.
The steps that take me to you
In the sunrise of days.
Your teething rage.
My lack of knowledge.
The angel locks I stole
From your infant kingdom.
Pikachu and little ponies.

I'm saving for you
The might of my country.
The tears of my country.
The saline mist that relaxes your nostrils.
The fine sands that massaged our toes.
My sandcastles that lacked imagination.

I'm saving for you
My Latin tongue.
The iron pot where empires
Mixed my race.
Cathedrals and Mosques.
Synagogues and temples.
The trees swayed by God's whispers.

God in all forms

I'm saving for you
I love you's before sunrise.
The, I'll miss you before bedtime.
The wind's pity on a humid August afternoon.
Time frozen still.
Photographs and poems.

But really,
Mati, I am saving for you
The best,
The first kisses on your forehead.
Your first steps.
Family hugs.
All my time for you.
Time to lose yourself.
Time to find yourself.
Hope of a long life.
A home.
Love.
The number of steps
In the sunset of time,
That will take me to you.

Love Poem

For: Ekaterina Ivanova Parra

Wrap your hair around me
And hold me fast.

If I strangle the blood orange moon with my stare
Or the blue birds poisoning each other's beaks,
If I flick
Tears at my bruised toes
Or the wrinkled edges on my face
Know,
That you are the light that makes way against
Shadows and muteness

You
The sunrise and sunset,
You that pull me towards
The ritual of cracking my bones to exorcise
The stress out of them.

The afternoon joy
That is what you are,
The spring in my legs,
The lift in my shoulders
That resuscitates my back,
The strength in my fingers
That press hard on my neck
To alleviate the crevices of pain.
You are religion,
Chapel and prayer.

You are the butterflies I sew to my gut
When you surprise me with that kiss you invent each day.

You,
the one that will stay forever embroidered
On fine mantel among lilies and pearls,
In the legend of my days.

WE

I was outside the Karl Marx theatre drinking Rum and Coke when a hyena walked up to me and urinated on me. It was mostly brown with gray spots on the legs. I started to pet it and it started licking my fingers. I was fascinated but felt a bit fearful and even wondered if I was going nuts. People looked disturbed. "It's not mine," I pleaded. "It came to me." "A hyena in a Cuba!" Some people started to scream in bewilderment- it stood on two legs and started licking my face. I felt that it was cleaning the spots of human defects that sometimes stained my face. An animal control officer came over to me and asked if all the vaccines were up to date. "It came to me," I said. The officer leaned forward to pet it and it bit off his finger, crushing his wrist in the process. He looked at me and started to cry. "My heart is broken," he said. "It was you that risked it," I said. He sobbed and then stood up and said: "What are you going to name it?" "Sweetheart," I said. "Jesus fucking Christ, this fucking country turns more and more bubble gum by the minute. Everywhere you turn there are people shouting, 'I love you' from balconies, or crying while plucking a rose, or calling savage animals Sweetheart, or, or, saying stuff like 'oops I did it again.' And then you have me, who always wanted to have a pet but makes a living killing them. Please forgive me if I start crying again." "That's fine," I said. "And let me tell you that soon a sweetheart will come your way." We said goodbye and walked towards the dark streets where the lights are turned off early in the evening, and the stench of trash snakes up the nose and pokes on the nostrils. I was not sure of the sanity of this reality but delighted myself in smearing and rolling in the creamy, caramelized syrup dripping from my heart.

THE LAST CUBAN MILITANT

My father is the last Cuban militant.
Raul Castro is shaking his ass to Hip-Hop,
And my father is still wearing his black beret, and green fatigues.
The Cafés are jammed with clean-shaven youths
Whose heads are gel addicts, and bodies crave
The sexy stroke of European soccer Jerseys.
A blind woman wants to discuss Rembrandt and Van Gogh with him,
And he doesn't even want to believe that the lips that gently kiss
His swollen feet under the covers is Christ pranking him.

The Americans will bomb us one day; I'll hide in the jungle.
The Europeans will have orgies on our beaches; I'll pretend I'm blind.
I have a limited-edition Makarov PM and a Mayakovsky poem,
I'll fight the war being advertised for the last 50 years.

Poem About Liars

The groom braids his mother's pleas in thin knots,
As if they were meant for a mannequin
Whose head had fallen off
With the weight of thick hair.

The bride baptizes her lover's image
In the dense darkness of her pupils,
Walks the church packed with inebriated Christians
With strawberry smudges on her teeth.

The crowd smells of sweat and booze
And, they smell each other's ears,
Flick sweat at one another and wear blindfolds,
Until the priest offers his dentures as a sacrament for all to lick.

The lens is broken argues the photographer.
No more pictures of curvy blondes wearing pink dresses.
No more crying mothers with raw onions on their plates.
We have only the promise of eternity to lie about.

Acknowledgments

"Power Outages" first appeared in *The Chicago Quarterly Review*

"T.V Show" first appeared in *Pear Drop Zine*

"No More I Love yous" first appeared in *Flapperhouse*

"Once Upon a Time" first appeared in *The Cimarron Review*

"IX Cuban Recollections" first appeared in *The Basalt Review*

"Martyr" first appeared in *The Indiana Review*

"Bacalao" first appeared in *The Cimarron Review*

"Animal" first appeared in *The Indiana Review*

"War Under Your Eyelids" first appeared in *The Ocotillo Review*

"At the Center of the Universe" first appeared in *REAL: Regarding Arts and Letters*

"Against the Red Light" first appeared in *The Lake*

"Flu in the Times of Allergies" first appeared in *Flapperhouse*

"Johnny on the Rocks" first appeared in *Flapperhouse*

"Waiting for Superman" first appeared in *4ink7*

"Roberto Giving Birth" first appeared in *Driftwood Press Review*

"Red Star" first appeared in *The Lake*

"Broken Spear" first appeared in *The Lake*

"Douchko" first appeared in *Flapperhouse*

"The Last Cuban Militant" first appeared in *Flapperhouse*

"We" first appeared in *4ink7*

"Poem about Liars" first appeared in *4ink7*

"IX Cuban Recollections" first appeared in *Basalt Review*

"Babalawo Ceremony" in the Central Dome first appeared in *Better Than Starbucks*

"Day and Night" and "Like This I Remain" were published in *The Avenue*